Finding Happiness in a Frustrating World

Jim Johnson, PT

Magnifying glass drawing by Eunice Johnson.

This edition published by
Dog Ear Publishing
4010 W. 86th Street, Ste H
Indianapolis, IN 46268

www.dogearpublishing.net

ISBN: 978-159858-748-7
Library of Congress Control Number: Applied For
This book is printed on acid-free paper.

Printed in the United States of America

Why Is The Print In This Book So Big?

People who read my books sometimes wonder why the print is so big in many of them. Some tend to think it's because I'm trying to make a little book bigger or a short book longer.

Actually, the main reason I use bigger print is for the same reason I intentionally write short books, usually under 100 pages–it's just plain easier to read and get the information quicker!

You see, the books I write address common, everyday problems that people of *all* ages have. In other words, the "typical" reader of my books could be a teenager, a busy housewife, a CEO, a construction worker, or a retired senior citizen with poor eyesight. Therefore, by writing books with larger print that are short and to the point, *everyone* can get the information quickly and with ease. After all, what good is a book full of useful information if nobody ever finishes it?

Contents

Introduction

As a physical therapist, I've been walking in and out of patient's rooms for nearly two decades and have often wondered how some people could be so sick, yet *still* remain so happy. Puzzled by this, I began researching the subject of happiness to try and find an explanation for what I was seeing. After sifting through piles of published research, I came across some pretty unexpected findings, and in the process, discovered why life can be more frustrating than happy–and what can be done about it. So, if you're as curious as I was.....

There once was a bright young physical therapist who worked in a large hospital. It was there that he spent his days busily traveling from room-to-room, between the various floors, teaching patients useful exercises and helping many to walk again. One of the things he enjoyed most about his job was the fact that he was able to work with lots of people from many different places.

As the young therapist gained more experience, he began to notice something unusual. Although many of his patients were very sick, and far from being in the best condition of their lives, not *all* of them were as depressed and miserable as one might expect. While no patient "enjoyed" being in the hospital, he would meet a few from time-to-time that were actually in good spirits despite their poor health.

To further confuse things, whether a patient was happy or not, seemed to have little to do with anything obvious such as how long they had been in the hospital or what their medical problems were. "I just don't understand how two patients can both be in bad shape, yet one depressed and the other so much happier," pondered the young therapist, "but I sure would like to know why."

On his next day off, the young therapist decided that it was finally time to get to the bottom of things. He felt like a good place to start was to find an expert in psychology, since it was the science of the mind and behavior. As there happened to be a well-known university nearby, he telephoned the psychology department to see if there was someone he could meet with.

"I know just the person you want to talk to," answered one of the secretaries. "He's one of our most knowledgeable professors on the subject of happiness."

"Great," said the young therapist, "that's *exactly* the kind of person I'm looking for. How soon can I see him?"

"You're in luck," said the secretary. "If you can make it today, he's available any time after ten o'clock."

"I'll see you at ten!" exclaimed the young therapist.

As he hung up the phone, he thought to himself, "At least if this professor can't give me *all* the answers I'm looking for, it will certainly be a good place to start." Not wasting any time, he quickly stuffed a pen and a small notebook in his pocket and headed out the door.

When the young therapist arrived at the professor's office, he found a well-groomed, elderly gentleman sitting behind a desk. "Come in," said the old professor. "Have a seat. You must be the physical therapist from the hospital."

"That's me," answered the young therapist as he sat down. "I'd like to thank you for meeting with me on such short notice."

"Not a problem," said the old professor. "I don't have any classes to teach today. What can I help you with?"

"Well, I'd like to ask you a few questions about happiness."

"Okay," smiled the old professor, "that's one of my favorite subjects. What do you want to know?"

"I guess my main problem is that I'm trying to figure out why some of my patients are so much happier than others."

"What exactly do you mean?" asked the old professor.

"Let me give you an example," began the young therapist. "I treated this elderly lady last week who just had her leg amputated as a complication of her diabetes. On top of that, she was also beginning to lose her vision. Now you'd think that a person in that kind of situation would be one of the most miserable and depressed patients you'd ever run into."

"Was she?"

"Definitely not. As a matter of fact, she was actually in what I would call 'a good mood.' The whole time I was trying to get her into the wheelchair, she was quite talkative, telling me all about her grandkids and the rest of her family. Let me also add that she was a retired maintenance worker and lived on a meager income."

"Go on," said the old professor as he leaned back in his chair.

"Okay, so that was in the morning. In the *afternoon,* I went to see a patient in the fancy wing of the hospital, a place reserved for VIP's. Now here's where it gets interesting. This particular patient was a lawyer who *also* had diabetes for many years and just had the same surgery as the elderly lady I saw in the morning—a leg amputation. And to top it all off, he too suffered from vision problems."

"Well, circulation and vision problems are pretty common in people with diabetes," stated the old professor. "Did he seem to be as happy as your other patient with the amputation?"

"Far from it," said the young therapist. "He was *really* depressed and would hardly talk. In fact, I barely got him sitting up at the edge of the bed."

"I see what you mean," said the old professor.

"You know," said the young therapist, "I guess I *could* just chalk it up to the fact that everybody responds differently to certain situations. However my gut tells me it's a little more complicated than that. After treating literally hundreds of patients over the years and consistently coming across individuals that seem to be happy no matter what they're faced with, I'm wondering just how this could be—*and what's their secret!*"

The old professor laughed. "I can see you've been giving this quite a bit of thought."

"I sure have. Do you think there's a logical explanation for what I've been seeing in the hospital?"

"I think I can shed a little light on things," said the old professor. "You know there's actually a lot of scientific research that helps explain who's happy and why."

"There is?" said the young therapist pulling his notebook out from his pocket.

"There sure is," replied the old professor. "But oddly enough, while happiness _is_ one of the most sought after things in the entire world, it's a subject most people know very little about."

"That does seem kind of odd," noted the young therapist.

The old professor continued. "And despite the fact that it's something literally _everyone_ wants, there's usually only one time people give it much thought."

"When's that?"

"When they're _unhappy._"

"That is true," said the young therapist nodding his head. "However I have to admit, when I go to work every day, the last thing on my mind is happiness."

The old professor laughed. "Well, you might not be aware of it," he said, "but much of what you do each day is for happiness. Just stop and think about how many of your day-to-day activities bring you immediate happiness _or_ a step closer to being happy."

"I guess you're right," admitted the young therapist. "Things like buying new clothes or eating chocolate do make me happy right away. On the other hand, things like going to work every day do contribute _indirectly_ to my happiness by earning me spending money–and keeping the bills paid."

"Those are all good examples," complimented the old professor. "And not only is happiness the main reason why we _do_ many things, but it's also the main reason why we _want_ most things."

"What do you mean?" said the young therapist, sounding a bit confused.

"Let's use a million dollars as an example," replied the old professor. "Now a lot of people wouldn't mind having that kind of money, would they?"

"I know I wouldn't," joked the young therapist.

"Well tell me this. Would you still want a million dollars *if you knew it wouldn't bring you any happiness*?"

The young therapist paused for a second. "Now wait a minute," he said. "In my mind, the two usually go together."

"That's true. But let's just pretend for a minute that I could separate the two and make it so that you could have a million dollars, but *no* happiness at all from it. Would you still want the money?"

"Well, if you put it like that," answered the young therapist, "I guess not. I mean after all, what good would a million dollars be if it didn't make me happy in some way or another?"

"That's exactly my point," explained the old professor. "Like you, most people wouldn't want a million dollars either if they knew it couldn't bring them any happiness. Why? *Simply because happiness is the main reason for wanting it in the first place.* This also holds true for many of the things we wish for."

"I see what you mean." said the young therapist.

"In many cases," continued the old professor, "people don't ever realize that happiness is indeed their 'ultimate pursuit'–probably because happiness naturally goes together with all the things we want in life. However when you sort things out, it becomes quite obvious. It's not really 'things' we're after, like good looks, wealth, a sports car, fame, a great vacation, or a dream home, but rather *the happiness* that these things could bring us."

"I guess I never thought of things quite like that," said the young therapist "Happiness *is* very important. Without it, many things we do and want just don't mean much at all."

"Can you imagine a world *without* it?" added the old professor.

The young therapist was now becoming quite interested in the old professor's ideas. He wrote:

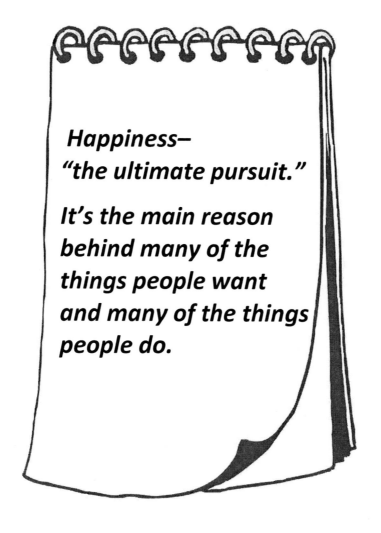

Happiness—
"the ultimate pursuit."

It's the main reason
behind many of the
things people want
and many of the things
people do.

"*So* you said there was a lot of scientific research on happiness?" asked the young therapist.

"That's right, much more than people are aware of," replied the old professor.

"But how do you go about studying something like happiness? I mean, is that even *scientifically* possible?"

"Absolutely," said the old professor. "While happiness may not seem 'concrete' enough to study, it is researched the same way we research other things we can't see or touch, like pain and depression."

"That makes sense," acknowledged the young therapist. "Come to think of it, researchers have been studying similar things for decades. So I suppose there's a 'happiness scale' they use to measure happiness?"

"There sure is," said the old professor, "or should I say there sure *are*. Like the many different types of depression and pain scales in use today, researchers have also developed lots of happiness scales to use over the years. Without going into a lot of details, let me just say that there are some really good ones out there that have been demonstrated to be both reliable *and* valid."

The young therapist paused to think for a moment. "Let me see if I remember this reliability and validity stuff correctly from school," he said. "If a happiness scale is *reliable*, that means that you'll be able to come up with the same result again if you went back and re-measured a person's happiness. And if a happiness scale is *valid*, then that means that it has been proven to actually measure what it's supposed to be measuring–happiness."

"You've got it," said the old professor.

"That's pretty impressive," said the young therapist. "But how does one go about proving that a happiness scale *actually* measures happiness? I mean how do you know people aren't just lying?"

"All good questions," said the old professor. "The way we find out if someone is really as happy as they say they are, is by comparing what they say to *other* indicators of happiness."

"Other indicators of happiness?"

"Sure. There are lots of things other than a person's self-report that can 'indicate' or tell us that someone is indeed a happy person. For example, one popular way is to have a subject's family or friends rate their happiness and then compare that to the subject's rating. In other words, if someone tells us that they are a happy person, do their friends and family see them as a happy person too?"

"That's pretty neat," said the young therapist listening attentively.

"There are many more indicators," said the old professor, "but to make a long story short, when we compare people's reports of how happy they are to other indicators of happiness, much research shows an agreement between the two. And this all means we have good reason to believe people when they say they are happy."

"I guess people aren't lying then," joked the young therapist.

The old professor grinned. "Apparently not."

"So with reliable and valid scales, I'm assuming a lot of the happiness research involves going out and surveying people to find out all kinds of things about happiness."

"That's *exactly* what they do. With a good way of measuring happiness in hand, one can then attempt to figure out who's happy and why."

"That's the stuff I want to know about," said the young therapist. Then he jotted:

Researchers have developed happiness scales that can measure happiness both validly and reliably.

The old professor leaned over and took a sip of his coffee. "Perhaps the best place to start is to first talk about things that have *very little* to do with your happiness."

"Okay," said the young therapist. "I'll bet money is at the top of the list. Everyone knows money can't buy happiness."

"Well I wouldn't go that far," said the old professor. "I know I'd be *very* happy if someone gave me a lot of money."

The young therapist laughed a little, wondering if it was a joke.

"I'm serious," said the old professor. "People are much happier when they suddenly come into money. Problem is, they don't *stay* that way."

"But why doesn't money keep a person happy?" asked the young therapist. "If it does at first, why not always?"

"Well, I don't think anyone can say with absolute certainty, but we do know a few things that can get in the way. For example, have you ever heard a song on the radio that you really, really liked?"

"Sure, everyone has."

"So what happened after you heard it over and over for about a month?"

"I got tired of it."

"And if you've ever bought a new car, you were pretty excited about it when you first got it, right?"

"Absolutely."

"And after two years?"

"Definitely not as excited as the day I bought it. Although I think at that point, the thought of having it all paid off made me pretty happy."

The old professor laughed. "What happens quite frequently is a process researchers call *adaptation*–and it's probably a big reason why money doesn't bring lasting happiness. Just like it gets old hearing a great song over and over, as would eating your favorite food for *every* meal, so does having a lot of money. At first, having more money brings a surge of happiness, there's no denying that. But after awhile, people 'adapt' to their new level of income and begin to consider it as normal. Then the increase in money isn't quite the big deal it was in the beginning."

"But is there any actual *evidence* showing that money doesn't make people any happier?"

"There sure is," said the old professor. "Happiness researchers have used several lines of research in order to arrive at the conclusion that money does not make one happier. One is by looking at a bunch of different countries and seeing if people in the wealthier ones are happier."

"What do they find?"

"Well, while they do find that people living in richer countries are happier than those living in poorer ones, there's a problem."

"What's that?"

"People in wealthier countries not only have more money, but they also have other positive things that could make them happier, such as better human rights."

"I see. So even though there's a strong connection between being happy and living in a wealthy country, you really can't be sure that it's due to people having more money *or* things like having better human rights."

"That's right."

"So what about when they look at the connection between happiness and wealth *within a single country*? Are the rich people happier? I would think that would give some better clues because within a given country, things like human rights are generally the same for everybody."

"That's good thinking," said the old professor, "and those studies have been done."

"And what do they show?"

"Only a *small* and *weak* connection between how much money you make and how happy you are. For instance, one interesting study compared 49 people who made over ten million dollars a year, to 62 randomly selected people that lived in the same areas as the rich people–but averaged only 36,000 dollars a year."

"So who was more satisfied with their life?

"The super-wealthy–*but only by about a point higher on a scale of 0 to 6!*"

"Wow."

"And that's only when researchers look at a relatively small number of subjects. Another study surveyed thousands of people in the United States and looked for a connection, or *correlation*, between income and happiness. They found it to be just .12."

".12 is pretty small considering '1' would be a perfect connection between being rich and being happy."

"That's right," confirmed the old professor. "And if you think that's just in the United States, researchers looking at *nineteen* nations came up with just a .13 connection between income and happiness."

"That's incredible," said the young therapist.

"It really is," said the old professor, "but the evidence gets even stronger. If there was a connection between money and happiness, wouldn't you suppose that people would be getting happier as they made more money each week?"

"One would think," said the young therapist.

"Well, when happiness researchers looked at people's income in the United States, Japan, and France from the years 1946 to 1990, they found that income increased tremendously in all three nations over this time period–even after accounting for taxes and inflation. For instance, in the United States, real income more than *doubled*."

"Hmm. So if income doubled, this means that people could theoretically buy twice as much stuff to make them happy."

"That's right."

"But did their happiness levels double as well?"

"Hardly," laughed the old professor. "Despite the fact that people's income in these three countries grew and grew and grew, *there was no increase in happiness levels*."

"Even more strong evidence that money doesn't buy happiness," noted the young therapist. "I guess even though I always knew that, I did think a *little* more money would make me happier."

"Well, let's talk about what happens when a person does come into more money. There was a study done once on lottery winners that looked at their happiness levels. These people were interviewed at least a month after winning, but no more than a year and a half after winning. Their level of happiness was then compared to a control group of people that lived in the same areas as the winners."

"And who was happier?"

"Nobody," smiled the old professor. "The study found that lottery winners and the people in the control group were *not* significantly different in how happy they were."

"That's hard to believe," said the young therapist.

"It is," agreed the old professor, "but as the research keeps *repeatedly* telling us, having a lot of money isn't all it's cracked up to be–and you certainly don't need it to be happy either. Direct evidence for this comes from studies where people around the world are surveyed to find out who's satisfied with their life and who's not."

"What do they find?"

"Plenty of people who *aren't* rich that are *very* satisfied with their lives."

"You mean they just go up and ask people how satisfied they are with their lives?"

"No, actually what they do is ask people to indicate how much they agree with the statement 'You are satisfied with your life' using a scale of 1 to 7."

"So I take it the higher the number, the more a person agrees that they are satisfied with their life?"

"That's right."

"So who's the most satisfied?"

"Not who you think. For instance millionaires from *Forbes* magazine's list of 'richest Americans' gave a life satisfaction rating of 5.8 out of 7, *as did the Pennsylvania Amish.* Even more amazing, when the Maasai were asked, they gave a 5.7 rating."

"Who's the Maasai?" asked the young therapist.

"A group of herding people who live in Africa," replied the old professor. "They live in huts made from dung *and have no running water or electricity.*"

The young therapist laughed. "Now wait a minute," he said. "You're telling me that there are people living in dung huts that are *almost* as happy as multi-millionaires?"

"It's all been scientifically documented," stated the old professor. "Pretty eye-opening research isn't it?"

"To say the least," agreed the young therapist. He then wrote:

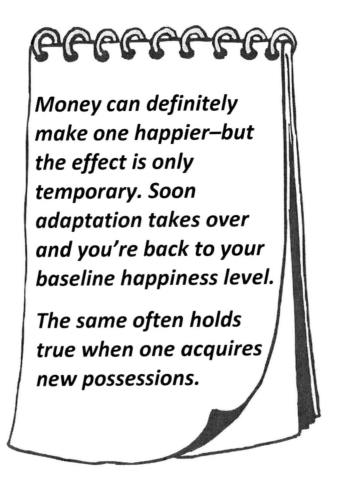

Money can definitely make one happier–but the effect is only temporary. Soon adaptation takes over and you're back to your baseline happiness level.

The same often holds true when one acquires new possessions.

"But now you've got me *really* curious," said the young therapist. "What other things have little to do with how happy a person is?"

"Your age," replied the old professor.

"No way," said the young therapist. "Now I would think that younger people would be the happiest."

"Yet *another* myth the happiness research has disproven," said the old professor.

"You're kidding me, right?"

"Not at all. Despite the fact that many unfortunate things can happen to people as they get older, like having more health problems, *happiness levels do not go down as people get older*. To sum up the research in this area, happiness levels have been found to either remain stable over the course of one's lifetime, or actually *increase*."

"That's just amazing," said the young therapist, "and certainly not what I expected at all. So just how do they go about finding this stuff out?"

"Well, two kinds of studies in particular have helped happiness researchers reach this conclusion. One is called a *cross-sectional study*. This is where you would go out and ask a bunch of people of all different ages how happy they are.

"A good example of this is a study where researchers surveyed 184 people between the ages of 18 and 94. They did this by having subjects wear beepers for a week during which time they were randomly paged five times a day. Then, when the beeper went off, subjects would have to write down in a booklet how happy they were on a scale of 1 to 7. Contrary to what most people think, the results showed that older people experienced positive emotions, such as happiness, *every* bit as often as the younger crowd."

"That's pretty clever," commented the young therapist.

The old professor continued. "But while these kinds of studies can show us differences in happiness that may or may not exist between old and young people, they aren't as good as *longitudinal studies*. Here, researchers take a group of people and keep track of their happiness levels over a *long* period of time."

"I see," said the young therapist. "So by using a longitudinal study, you can actually see how people's happiness levels change over the years as they grow older."

"Yep," said the old professor. "And one of the best longitudinal studies published actually followed 2,804 people from 1971 to 1994."

"That's twenty-three years!" exclaimed the young therapist. "How old were the people when they started the study?"

"They varied all the way from 15 to 90 years old."

"Wow," said the young therapist. "So let me guess, happiness levels remained pretty stable over time?"

"That's right," stated the old professor, "and there are *more* studies that show the same thing. Apparently getting older isn't as bad as everyone thinks it is."

The young therapist noted:

Long-term studies show that happiness levels either stay the same or increase as one gets older.

"That's funny," pondered the young therapist. It just seems to me that as people get older and have more health problems, they would have to be less happy."

"Well, let's talk about health and happiness for a minute," said the old professor. "First of all, good health is related to being happy, and bad health is related to being unhappy. *But, this health-happiness connection only holds true when the person is the one judging whether their health is good or bad.* In other words, if a person sees themselves as being in good health, then they will tend to be happy. However if they think of themselves as being in poor health, then they will tend to be *un*happy."

"I see," said the young therapist, "So it's really a person's *self-rated health* that correlates with their happiness levels, not necessarily the doctor's diagnosis or what condition they're in according to a medical chart."

"Exactly," said the old professor. "Concrete or 'objective' measurements of a person's health, like what disease they have, how well they move around, or how many arms and legs they have, simply *don't* tell you a lot about how happy a person really is."

"It's very surprising that *objective health* has little to do with happiness," stated the young therapist. "Is there any good research to support this?"

"Yes," said the old professor. "One good example is a study that followed about 375 men and women from 1970 to 1976. Every couple of years, researchers would find out how they rated their own health, as well as and how happy they were. Additionally, objective health measures were collected which included the number of doctor's visits and operations someone had, as well as how many times and how long they had been in the hospital. At the end of this longitudinal study, researchers were unable to find *any* direct effect of objective health on a person's happiness."

"So then things like how many times they had to go see a doctor or how many operations they underwent had nothing to do with how happy they were?"

"Nope, and other studies have found similar results. Another notable one followed several hundred people over a period of years. This time, however, they collected data on, happiness levels, how healthy people were according to a doctor's opinion, and how healthy people were in their *own* opinion."

"Let me guess," said the young therapist, "How healthy the doctor thought they were had nothing to do with how happy they were."

"Right again," said the old professor. "As the research keeps showing us, when it comes to health and happiness, it's how healthy *you* think you are that really matters."

"Just amazing," said the young therapist. "Common sense tells me that poor health should automatically mean less happiness."

"You would think," said the old professor, "but that's obviously *not* the case. I remember a study once that took a group of people that were sixty or more years old and recorded how happy they were and how physically disabled they were. Five to six years later, when researchers re-examined subjects, they found that although subjects were significantly *more* disabled, their happiness levels stayed the same."

"It's hard to argue with studies like that," said the young therapist.

"And along the same lines," said the old professor, "another study I know of investigated legally blind people to find out just how happy they are."

"Sounds like another good study," said the young therapist.

"It was," said the old professor, "particularly because this one included a *control group* made up of people who *could* see. You really need that comparison to know for sure whether blind people are actually happier, or unhappier, than anyone else."

"So what did the study find?"

"Believe it or not," said the old professor, "the researchers found that the blind people were actually a little happier than the control group of people who could see."

The young therapist was silent for a moment, not sure what to think. "Are you sure you're not just making this stuff up?" he said.

The old professor smiled. "I can assure you I'm not," he said. "All the research we've been talking about has been published in well-known academic journals. I'll give you all the references when we're done so you can look them up and read them for yourself if you want to."

"Thanks," said the young therapist, "I'd really like that. You know, it's just that it's so hard to believe that people can adapt so well to just about any health problem."

"Well, human beings can certainly adapt to *a lot* of medical problems," said the old professor, "but I don't want to leave you with the impresion that they can adapt to illnesses and disabilities of *every* kind. Happiness research has found a few medical conditions that can definitely knock the wind out of a person's happiness. Working in a hospital, I'll bet you can guess what some of them are. "

"I think I know one of them," said the young therapist. "People with spinal cord injuries?"

"Unfortunately you're right." said the old professor. "There are many studies that have compared people with spinal cord injuries to control groups of non-disabled people–and found that people with spinal cord injuries just aren't quite as happy."

"Hmm," said the young therapist thinking, "I guess you could sum up health and happiness like this. The impact of your health on your happiness depends on how *you* see your medical condition. However, when a medical condition is very severe, like with a spinal cord injury, it certainly can affect your level of happiness. But, for the most part, people can pretty much adapt to a wide range medical problems that they get during their lifetime–the many studies on happiness, aging, and disability have definitely proven that."

"I think that sums up the connection between health and happiness pretty well," commented the old professor.

The young therapist quickly wrote down:

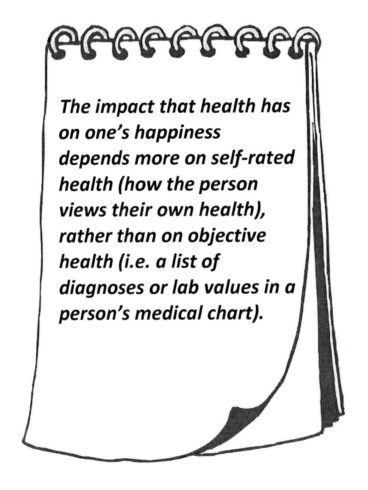

The impact that health has on one's happiness depends more on self-rated health (how the person views their own health), rather than on objective health (i.e. a list of diagnoses or lab values in a person's medical chart).

"So what else has little to do with people's happiness according to the research?"

"Whether you're male or female," answered the old professor.

"Oh," said the young therapist. "So men and women have similar levels of happiness?"

"That's what they've found," replied the old professor. "A good example of the research in this area includes surveys conducted in sixteen nations of more than 160,000 people. Researchers found that men and women did *not* differ substantially in their happiness levels. This is a particularly good study because it looked at a wide range of people across many different cultures from around the world. Other studies have also come to the same conclusion."

"What about intelligence?" asked the young therapist.

The old professor laughed. "So you're wondering if smarter people are happier than dumber people?"

"Just a thought," chuckled the young therapist.

"Well, actually there has been some research done on happiness and intelligence," said the old professor. "But by now, I'll bet you can *probably* figure out what they've found."

"Let me guess," said the young therapist, "no connection."

The old professor smiled. "In one study, researchers had 269 subjects rate their happiness levels, as well as take tests of their spatial, verbal and math abilities. As you have correctly guessed, the study showed that how smart a person is has *very little* to do with how happy they are. And here again, there are many other studies that have also come to this same conclusion."

The young therapist made a few more notes:

-men and women have similar levels of happiness

-intelligence has little to do with how happy a person is

Suddenly a puzzled look came over the young therapist's face.

"What's wrong?" asked the old professor.

"This happiness research is sure throwing me for a loop."

"What do you mean?" asked the old professor.

"Well, according to the studies you've been telling me about, if I were to try and figure out why one of my patients was so happy most of the time, it really wouldn't help me much to know if their income was four *or* six figures a year, if they drove a Chevy *or* a Mercedes, whether they wore a suit *or* overalls to work, if they were seventeen *or* seventy, male *or* female, or even if they had a fifth grade education *or* a degree from Harvard."

"That's all true," said the old professor. "But don't give up just yet on your quest to find out why some people are happier than others. Remember, solving a puzzle also involves knowing where the pieces *don't* go. That's why I chose to discuss things that have little to do with long-term happiness first."

Feeling a little more optimistic about things, the young therapist was now ready with more questions. "Since you've told me about some of the things that have very little to do with a person's happiness, I guess the next thing I need to know is, *what does?*"

"Well, happiness researchers have pinpointed at least three things that clearly contribute to people's long-term happiness levels," said the old professor. "One of them is your genetics."

"Really?" said the young therapist. "How do we know that?"

"*Twin studies* have given us a lot of information about this," answered the old professor.

"Twin studies?" said the young therapist.

"That's right. Twin studies help us sort out if it's your genes that have a lot do with a certain behavior like happiness, or if it's just the environment you live in. They've been used a lot in depression and alcoholism research, so why not happiness?"

"How do they work?" asked the young therapist.

"Well in a nutshell," said the old professor, "researchers first locate literally *hundreds* of pairs of twins to study. Then they gather and compare information from pairs of *identical* twins, as well as from pairs of *fraternal* twins."

"So why do they need both identical *and* fraternal twins?"

"Because researchers figure out how big a role genes play in happiness by comparing the similarities and differences in identical twins and fraternal twins. Remember that identical twins share 100% of their genes. Fraternal twins, on the other hand, share only about 50% of their genes–and serve as an important control group for comparing twin similarity."

"I see. So if genes are really a factor in one's happiness, a twin study should find more similarity in happiness levels between two *identical* twins, than between two *fraternal* twins."

"Correct," answered the old professor, "and that's exactly what *many* twin studies on happiness have found. However, keep in mind that genetics plays *only a part* in determining your long-term happiness levels. While one's genetic make-up is clearly a significant factor, it is but one factor and does *not* in and of itself entirely decide how happy you will be. I like to think of long-term happiness levels as being more genetically *influenced*, not necessarily genetically *fixed*."

"So it's kind of like a person's weight. Some people are born with a really slow metabolism and have a tendency to gain weight easily. However even those people can maintain a healthy weight if they eat properly and exercise."

"Weight is a perfect analogy," said the old professor.

The young therapist wrote:

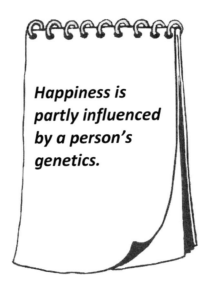

Happiness is partly influenced by a person's genetics.

"And speaking of things other than your genes that contribute to your long-term happiness, that brings me to *circumstances*."

"Circumstances?" said the young therapist. "What exactly do you mean?"

"I'm talking about things, good or bad, that just 'happen' to a person as they're living life. Some examples could be the day a person got into a car accident and ended up becoming paralyzed *or* the day they just happened to run into the love of their life."

"That makes sense," said the young therapist.

"It does," agreed the old professor, "and there's even been some happiness research to back up this common sense."

"Really?" said the young therapist. "It seems like that would be a hard study to do. I mean in order to know if a life circumstance significantly changed someone's happiness level for a long period of time, wouldn't you have to know how happy they were before, during, and after an *unexpected* event?"

"You would,' said the old professor, "and that's exactly what researchers have done."

"You're kidding?"

"Not at all. For instance one longitudinal study followed over 24,000 individuals for *fifteen* years. It found that many widows and widowers were less happy for years after their spouse died. Other life circumstances that can be unexpected, such as becoming divorced or unemployed, have also been shown in studies to result in long-lasting changes in your happiness."

"You know even though that's common sense," said the young therapist, "I guess it is good that they've done those kinds of studies–it's just proof positive that genetics doesn't entirely account for a person's happiness. If they did, things like getting divorced or having your spouse die wouldn't affect your happiness levels for very long. These studies show that some circumstances really can change things."

The professor shook his head in agreement. The young therapist wrote:

Happiness is partly determined by a person's circumstances.

"I was wondering something though," said the young therapist. "Didn't you say that there were are at least *three* things that clearly contribute to a person's long-term happiness?"

"You are paying attention," said the old professor smiling. "The third one is *intentional activity*."

"Oh," said the young therapist. "So those would be things we do *on purpose* to try and make ourselves happier, like going on vacation or buying something new."

"Well, those types of intentional activities will certainly increase our happiness," said the old professor, "but remember, right now we're talking about increasing our *long-term* happiness. The things you've mentioned, like buying something new for yourself, usually results in just a *temporary* boost of happiness."

"But why can't you use a bunch of these 'temporary happiness boosters' all the time to stay happy?" asked the young therapist.

"That's probably the most commonly used method," replied the professor, "but it's not a good way to go about finding *long-term* happiness."

"Why not?"

"Because of the process of *adaptation* that we talked about earlier. Things like a new house, a new car, a new pair of shoes, or eating at a new restaurant *will* make you happy–but only for a limited amount of time. Once you get used to them, or 'adapt' to them, the happiness fades away–leaving you right back where you started. Of course you then go looking for something else to give you another temporary boost, and the whole process keeps repeating itself–*never leaving you with lasting happiness*."

"I see what you mean about that not being the best way," said the young therapist. "It kind of reminds me of being on a treadmill–you put forth effort but you don't go anywhere!"

"Exactly my point," said the professor. "Now that's not to say that temporary happiness boosters don't have their place. For instance, say you've had a hard day at work that's left you stressed out and frustrated. Well, certainly there's nothing wrong with going out for some comfort food or doing some relaxing shopping if that's your thing. *Just know that if you're really looking to find happiness over the long run, that's not the best way to go about it.*"

Listening attentively, the young therapist busily recorded a few more notes:

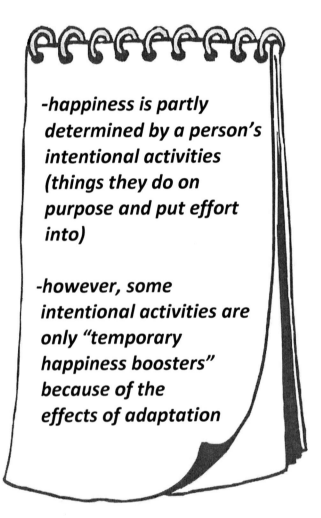

-happiness is partly
determined by a person's
intentional activities
(things they do on
purpose and put effort
into)

-however, some
intentional activities are
only "temporary
happiness boosters"
because of the
effects of adaptation

"*So* I'm thinking there's not much hope for some of us," said the young therapist.

"What do you mean?" laughed the old professor.

"Well, just think about it. You said there were three things that contributed to long-term happiness. The first was genetics, and there's not much you can do to change your genetics is there?"

"Not really."

"Well, that's great if you're gifted with a 'happy' personality, but what if you've got crappy genetics?"

"I guess you're just stuck with them," grinned the old professor.

"Exactly. Now the second thing you said that contributes to long-term happiness are your circumstances."

"Right."

"Well, since those are things that just 'happen' to you, there's not much you can do about luck."

"True," agreed the old professor.

"And the last thing that contributes to long-term happiness is intentional activity–which *is* something we can control. However as you have pointed out, that only makes us happy temporarily. So, the way I see it, trying to find lasting happiness is a lost cause."

"I have to admit," said the old professor, "With two of the three things that contribute to our happiness out of our control, things do look bad. However, we're *not quite* through talking about intentional activity yet."

"Well what more is there to say about intentional activity?"

"A lot," said the old professor. "Believe it or not, researchers have found that certain kinds of intentional activity can actually bring about long-term happiness."

"Really? What are they?"

"Well, my personal favorite is setting and working towards a personal goal."

"But does that *really* work?" asked the young therapist.

"It does if you select the right kind of goal."

"That almost sounds too good to be true," said the young therapist skeptically. "Are there any controlled trials proving this?"

"There sure are," said the old professor. "One I like in particular to tell people about took a bunch of volunteers and randomly assigned them to be in one of two groups. The first one was the control group. Subjects in it just sat on a waiting list for ten-weeks. In contrast, those assigned to the *second* group worked on developing a specific and measurable goal that they could reach, or at least make good progress towards, within a ten-week period."

"So this is a *randomized* controlled trial," said the young therapist. "Those kinds of studies are the highest form of proof in medicine that a treatment really works."

"That's correct," said the old professor. "And a randomized controlled trial carries *a lot of weight* when you're trying to prove that something's effective."

"So what happened?"

"Well, not only did the group that set and worked towards a goal become much happier than the control group, but, *they actually maintained their happiness gains when researchers checked on them thirty-weeks later!*"

"That's over seven months!" exclaimed the young therapist.

"Pretty impressive, isn't it?" said the old professor.

"I'll say."

The old professor continued. "Other controlled trials have also shown similar results. In another study, a group of 177 subjects served as a control group that did nothing, while another group of 117 worked on setting and achieving personal goals."

"Let me guess," said the young therapist, "People in the goal group made greater gains in happiness than those in the control group?"

"That's exactly what they found," said the old professor. *"Let me also add that this jump in happiness was maintained six months later."*

The young therapist shook his head and said, "Those are some amazing results."

"If you like," offered the old professor, "I'd be happy to discuss some more studies with you…"

"Ah, that's okay," said the young therapist, "Definitely personal goal setting is one kind of intentional activity that *can* increase happiness–and for a pretty good while." He then noted:

Controlled trials have proven that personal goal setting can produce long-term happiness.

"I'm curious though, so all you have to do is just set a goal and go for it?"

"Not exactly," said the old professor. "When it comes to goals and happiness, *what* you're going after and *why* you're going after it makes all the difference in the world."

"What does that mean?" asked the young therapist.

"It means that the best goals for increasing your long-term happiness meet two main requirements," explained the old professor. "The first is that they should be *self-concordant* goals."

"Self-concordant?"

"Yes. A self-concordant goal is one that represents your actual interests and values. This is the opposite of a *non*-concordant goal which is pursued because you feel like you 'have to'."

"I see, so self-concordant goals are ones that you really enjoy and believe in."

"That's correct," said the old professor. "Tell you what. Let me give you a quick test to help show the differences between the two. I'll give you an example of a goal, and you tell me if it's self-concordant or non-concordant."

"Okay."

"A child picks the goal of learning to play the violin because they love music and have always wanted to learn how."

"Self-concordant."

"Right! How about this? A child picks the goal of learning to play the violin because their parents want them to."

"Non-concordant."

"Yep. What about picking the goal of going to bible study regularly because you're afraid of what others might think of you if you didn't?"

"Non-concordant."

"Right again! Okay, one last example. What about picking the goal of going to bible study regularly because it seems enjoyable and interesting to you?"

"That's easy, self-concordant."

"I think you've got the hang of things," said the old professor. "I know it's kind of a corny test, but the point you need to be aware of is that two people can choose the exact same goal, yet have two *entirely* different reasons for pursuing it. *This difference is very crucial in determining if the goal will make you happy or not.*"

"So could you say that people who have self-concordant goals are much happier than people who have non-concordant goals?"

"According to much research, absolutely. Many studies have taken large groups of subjects and asked them to pick some goals to work on over a certain period of time–usually months. Each goal is then rated how self-concordant it is, and the happiness of each subject is measured before and after the study. *Time after time*, it's the people who choose and work towards the self-concordant goals that are found to be the happiest."

"That's pretty interesting."

"It really is," continued the old professor, "and what's even more interesting is the fact that this link that has been found between self-concordant goals and happiness seems to be a *universal* one."

"So it applies to everyone?"

"Well, at least *a lot* of us," said the old professor. "A multi-cultural study has shown that."

"What did that involve?"

"Well, basically, researchers survey individuals from around the world to see if it still holds true that people with self-concordant goals are the happiest."

"And that's what they found?"

"As a matter of fact, they found that having self-concordant goals predicted happiness within *every* culture studied."

The young therapist scribbled down:

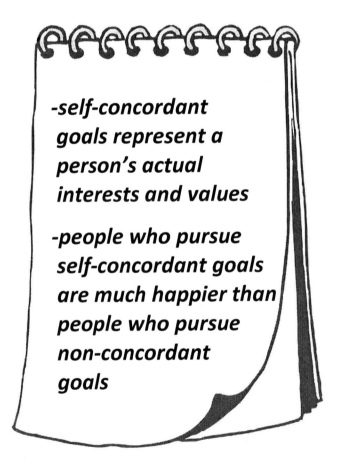

-self-concordant goals represent a person's actual interests and values

-people who pursue self-concordant goals are much happier than people who pursue non-concordant goals

"Okay, I'm a believer!" smiled the young therapist. "But tell me, if being self-concordant is the *first* main requirement for a personal goal to bring long-term happiness, what's the second?"

"It needs to be an *intrinsic* goal."

"What's that?"

"Intrinsic goals are ones that are in and of themselves satisfying to pursue. For instance, they could involve personal growth, where you're pursuing an interest, a 'calling', or maybe just trying to better understand yourself. Community involvement, where your aim is to improve the world in some way. Physical health, where you're attempting to be healthy and free of illness. Or maybe affiliation, in which you're working towards having a more satisfying relationship with your family or friends. Of course there are more, but these are the major categories that researchers have used in studies."

"So I guess if there are intrinsic goals, then there must be *extrinsic* goals as well?"

"Yep. But unlike intrinsic goals, extrinsic goals are generally *not* satisfying in and of themselves. Instead, they are more focused on getting rewards and praise. For instance they could involve financial success, where you want to make a lot of money. Popularity, where your aim is to be well-known, famous, and admired. Or maybe image, in which you are focusing on having an attractive physical appearance and being in style."

"Those are pretty different from intrinsic goals," noted the young therapist.

"They are," said the old professor. "Let me give you another quick test to further highlight the differences between the two. Like we did before, I'll give you a *general* example of an intrinsic or extrinsic of goal, and you tell me which one it is. Ready?"

"Ready."

"I will be famous and admired by many people."

"Extrinsic."

"Correct. I will get a job that pays a lot and own many nice things."

"Extrinsic."

"Yep. How about 'I will gain insight as to why I do the things I do'?"

"Intrinsic."

"Good. What about 'I will help to make the world a better place?'"

"Intrinsic."

"Right. A few more. I will have a caring relationship with someone."

"Intrinsic."

"How about 'I want to look good and attractive to other people'?"

"Definitely extrinsic."

"Pretty good, you haven't missed yet! Okay, one last goal. How about 'I will be physically healthy'?"

"Probably intrinsic."

"Not bad!" complimented the old professor.

"Thanks," said the young therapist. "However I have a question."

"What's that?"

"Well, I can see how working on an intrinsic goal would make you happier than working on extrinsic ones, but you know me by now, is there any research that actually *proves* this?"

"Plenty," said the old professor. "For instance one cross-sectional study took several hundred subjects, had them list their goals, and then measured their happiness levels. Sure enough, the people who were happiest of all were the ones that pursued the *intrinsic* rather than the extrinsic goals. Also highly notable, is the fact that when researchers study people from many different cultures around the world, they repeatedly find that those individuals who focus and place more importance on *extrinsic* goals tend to have *lower* well-being and happiness."

The young therapist busily jotted down:

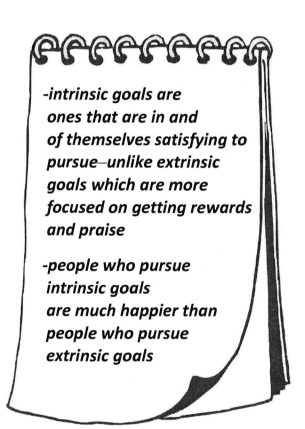

-intrinsic goals are
ones that are in and
of themselves satisfying to
pursue—unlike extrinsic
goals which are more
focused on getting rewards
and praise

-people who pursue
intrinsic goals
are much happier than
people who pursue
extrinsic goals

The young therapist paused for minute. "You know," he said, "I was just thinking, could an extrinsic goal still be okay to pursue if you're pursuing it for a self-concordant reason?"

"Good question. So you're wondering if it's okay to go after an extrinsic goal, such as making a lot of money, *if* you have a self-concordant reason, such as you really enjoy it?"

"Yeah. Say you really enjoy and believe in making a lot of money and set that as your goal–will you still be happy?"

"That's actually an important issue that researchers have addressed," said the old professor.

"What did they find?"

"Well, first of all, what you pursue, an intrinsic versus an extrinsic goal, and why you pursue it, for self-concordant versus non-concordant reasons *both* matter–*simply because each one makes its own individual contribution to the happiness that a goal can bring you.* In other words, they have an additive effect."

"I get it. So to get the most happiness out of a goal, make sure it's an intrinsic *and* a self-concordant goal."

"Correct. And to answer your question, the person who enjoys his goal of making a lot of money, according to the research, will probably *not* be as happy as the person who enjoys his goal of donating fifty-dollars each month to charity."

"So then I guess it's best to just avoid extrinsic goals altogether, huh?"

"Well, let's put it this way. Intrinsic goals will definitely make you happier than extrinsic goals–and they're what you should shoot for when trying to maximize your happiness. However realistically, if you happen to have a few extrinsic goals now and then, it's probably not the worst thing in the world—as long as they don't begin to dominate and 'take over' your whole goal system."

"Okay, tell me if I've got this right. When all is said and done, if you want to be happier, setting and working towards goals has been *proven* to work according to controlled trials. And when it comes to goals, pick those that are both *intrinsic* and *self-concordant* for maximum happiness."

"That's right," confirmed the old professor. The young therapist then added to his notes:

-what people pursue and why they pursue it both matter because each one contributes individually to how happy a goal can make them

-for maximum happiness, make sure that a goal is both self-concordant and intrinsic

Suddenly the old professor laughed.

"What's so funny?" asked the young therapist.

"I just realized something."

"What's that?"

"You've just summed up *piles* of studies and *years* of research in just a few sentences!"

The young therapist laughed. Glancing down at his watch, he checked the time. "Wow," he said, "it's getting late. I should probably be letting you go."

"Before you go," said the old professor, "do you think you have an answer to the question that brought you here?"

The young therapist smiled. "I think I do," he said. "I'm guessing the answer lies somewhere in the three things that contribute to a person's happiness–genetics, circumstances, and intentional activities. Obviously the patients I'm seeing in the hospital who seem happy no matter what they're faced with are genetically gifted with a high happiness "set-point." So, they're happier than most even though their circumstances are not good. Also, a lot of these happy individuals, more often than not, seem "intrinsically oriented" in that they seem to be more focused on things like their families and relationships, rather than their bank accounts and possessions."

"I would tend to agree with you," said the old professor as he leaned over to shake the young therapist's hand. "I think you definitely know a lot more about happiness than when you first walked in."

"I sure do–thanks to you."

"Always glad to share what I know," said the old professor. He then handed the young therapist a small pile of research studies as they walked out the door.

The young therapist spent the next week pouring over the stack of studies that the old professor had been kind enough to give him. As unbelievable as some of the happiness facts seemed, *all* the information that the old professor had talked about was well-documented in the studies.

The young therapist got to thinking about how useful all this information was–and what a shame it would be to let it stay buried within the pages of academic journals. "Now that I know a little more about the in's and out's of happiness," he said to himself, "I think I'll put this knowledge to good use." And so, he decided to try and increase his own happiness through goal setting.

Recalling what he had learned from the old professor, the young therapist knew that if a goal was to bring him maximum happiness, it must be both a *self-concordant* as well as an *intrinsic* goal.

After some reflective thinking, he wrote down his first goal:

"In two months, I will be spending one more hour a week doing things with my family."

The young therapist looked at the goal he had just written. He was satisfied with it because it met all the requirements of a goal that could make him happier. It was self-concordant because it reflected his actual interests and values. It was also intrinsic because it would be satisfying in and of itself for him to pursue.

Over the next few months, the young therapist continued working on his goal, and in time, reached it. "The old professor *was* right," he thought to himself, "Pursuing the right goals really can make you happier. And now that I've achieved my first one, I think I'll pick another one and just keep repeating the process."

So well did this goal setting process work for the young therapist that he decided to come up with a step-by-step plan so that others could increase their happiness as well…

Step 1
Pick a general area of your life that you want to improve.

There are endless goals you can set, so where does one begin? By first deciding on a *general area* that you'd like to improve on the most. Use the following pie chart to get a few ideas…

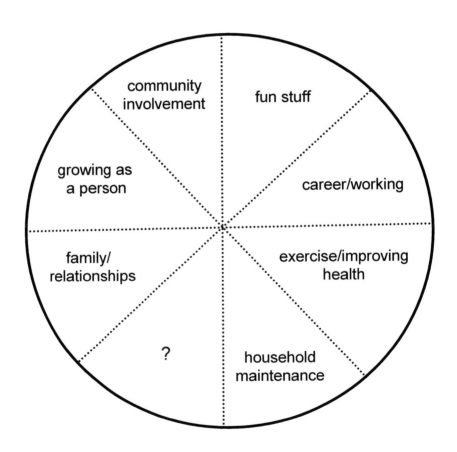

Step 2
Get a little more specific.

Once you've decided on a general area of your life that you want to improve, it's time to get a little more focused. In the pages that follow, find the general area you just picked in Step 1, and use the questions in that category to help you decide on something more specific to work on…

Fun Stuff

- Are there any new sports you'd like to learn to play?
- What hobbies might you be interested in getting involved in?
- Is there an area you feel you could write a book or article about?
- Was there ever a musical instrument you wanted to play?
- Are there any places you've ever wanted to visit?
- What would be your idea of a dream vacation?
- Are there any clubs you would like to join?
- What books would you like to read?
- Are there any new languages you'd like to learn?
- What new types of foods would you like to try?
- Have you ever had an idea for a new invention?

Career/Working

- What skills could you learn that would progress your career?
- Are there any certifications that would advance your career?
- What about joining a professional organization in your field?
- Are there any courses or degrees that will enhance your career?
- Are there any journals or books that would help keep you more up-to-date in your field?
- What is your ideal job?
- Is there another place you'd rather be employed at?

Exercise/Improving Health

- Ideally, how many times a week would you like to work out?
- How many hours of rest do you wish you could get each night?
- Are there any bad eating habits you'd like to give up?
- Are there any good exercise habits you'd like to start?
- Ideally, how much would you want to weigh?
- Do you want to be stronger or have toner muscles?
- Would you like to have more stamina and energy during the day?
- Would you like be more flexible?
- Do you get regular dental and medical check-ups?
- Would joining a gym or getting a personal trainer improve your exercise habits?
- Are there any health problems you have that you would like to learn more about?

Household Maintenance

- Is your house as clean as you would like it to be?
- Is your yard landscaped the way you would like it?
- Ideally, what projects around the house would you like to see get done?
- Is your house as safe as you would like it to be?
- Is there anything you could do to reduce your power bills and make you home run more efficiently?
- What could you do to improve the value of your house?
- How could you use the space more efficiently in your house?
- Would paying your bills on-line be easier and save you time?
- Would a monthly budget give you more peace of mind?
- Have you considered starting a household emergency fund?
- Are there any debts you'd like to get rid of?

Family/Relationships

- What friends or relatives would you like to see that you haven't seen in awhile?
- Have you considered organizing a family reunion?
- Do you see your good friends as often as you'd like to?
- Are there any people that are bad influences on you that you need to see less of?
- Would you like to get to know your neighbors better?
- Have you considered starting a weekly family get-together such as going to the movies or playing a sport?
- Have you considered starting a family tree?
- Are there any skills you have that you could teach your significant other or children?
- What kinds of things could you do to improve communication with your children or significant other?
- Ideally, what kind of relationship would you like to have with your children or significant other?
- Is there anything special you'd like to plan to do or get for your children or significant other for their next birthday or anniversary?
- Are there any small things you could do for your children or significant other on a regular basis to show them how much you love them?
- Have you considered planning a second honeymoon, or even a quick getaway, for your significant other?
- Are there any new and exciting things you and your significant other could do together in terms of hobbies, activities, or vacations?
- Are there any things you used to enjoy doing with your significant other that you haven't done regularly in awhile?
- If you don't have a significant other, what activities could you get involved with to meet new people?

Growing as a Person

- If you could get rid of one *bad* habit, what would it be?
- If you could acquire one *good* habit, what would it be?
- What are some of the things you've done that have made you feel good about yourself and could you do them regularly?
- Are there any past mistakes you've made that you need to forgive yourself for?
- Are there people that have helped you along the way that you could thank?
- Do you have any fears or phobias you would like to overcome?
- Do you need to manage your time better?
- Do you have a problem putting things off?
- Are there any areas of your life you feel that you need to be more responsible or assertive in?
- Have you considered setting aside some quiet time every day?
- If you were assured success at doing one thing, what would it be?
- Would you learn something new by reading books or watching programs that have much different points of view from your own?
- If you were stranded somewhere and had five minutes left to live, who would you call and what would you say?
- Is there any "unfinished business" that you need to take care of?
- Is there something new you've always wanted to learn about?
- Are there any steps you could take to simplify your life?
- What things make you feel peaceful inside? Can you do any of them on a regular basis?
- What kinds of things do you want to be remembered for?
- If you could write your own obituary, what would it say?
- What could you do to develop your religious beliefs?
- Are there any religious places you've always wanted to visit?
- What things can you do to express your spiritual beliefs?

Community Involvement

- Are there items in your house you aren't using that you could give to the poor?
- Do you have any clothes you don't wear anymore that you could give to charity?
- Is it possible for you to donate some of your money regularly to a good cause?
- Are there any charitable organizations that you could donate some of your time to?
- Have you considered sponsoring a child through the mail?
- How about recycling your used bottles and plastics?
- Are there any political or social issues interesting to you that you could get involved in?
- Have you considered running for a public office to help make a difference?
- If you could make one contribution to mankind, what would it be?

So how'd you do? Keep in mind that these questions are *not* meant to give you a comprehensive list of ideas–but rather a few suggestions to get you thinking.

If you can't seem to come up with something to work on right away, don't worry. Just take your time, and with some honest, reflective thinking, an idea for a goal *will* come. Consider talking with others or using additional resources too such as the internet.

Step 3
Write down your goal.

Up to now we've been just *thinking* about a goal to work on–now it's time to actually write one down. But before we do that, we need to make sure the goal includes a few things so it can bring *maximum* happiness...

1. *Your goal should be self-concordant*, meaning that it represents your actual interests and values. According to the research, here are some ways to know if your goal is a self-concordant goal:

   - you are pursuing your goal because you believe it's an important goal to have

   - while others may have suggested your goal, you endorse it freely and value it for personal reasons

   - you are pursuing your goal because of the fun and enjoyment it can provide you

   - while there were many good reasons to pick this goal, the main reason is simply your interest in the experience itself

You can also tell if you've picked a self-concordant goal if your goal does **not** have any of the qualities of a *non-concordant* goal, such as:

   - you picked your goal because somebody else wanted you to or because your situation seems to demand it

   - you probably wouldn't have picked the goal if you didn't get some kind of reward, praise, or approval for it

   - you picked your goal because you would feel ashamed, guilty, or anxious if you didn't

2. *Your goal should be intrinsic*, meaning that it is in and of itself satisfying to pursue. According to the literature, intrinsic goals typically involve things such as:

- trying to understand one's own self
- pursuing one's own interests and callings
- being closely connected to family and friends
- trying to improve the state of the community/world
- physical fitness (health)

You can also tell if you've picked an intrinsic goal by making sure it does **not** resemble an *extrinsic* goal, which deals with things such as:

- making a lot of money
- acquiring many possessions
- having an attractive physical appearance
- being well-known and admired/gaining status

3. *Your goal should also be measurable.*

- if it isn't, how will you know when you've reached your goal? "I will meet two new people a week over the summer" is much better than "I will meet lots of new people over the summer."

- just how measurable should a goal be? Measurable enough so that *you* will know without a doubt when the goal has been met.

4. *Make sure you include a specific time frame for your goal to be accomplished.*

Okay. You've thought about a general area of your life that you want to improve and you've come up with something specific to work on. So, in the space below, write a self-concordant, intrinsic goal, that is measurable and includes a target date to be accomplished:

"_____"

Step 4
Make a plan.

Now that you have a goal to work on, it's time to come up with a detailed plan that will enable you to reach it. Answering the questions below will help you to come up with one…

- How do you plan to reach your goal? _____

  _____

  _____

- What must you *specifically* do to reach your goal? _____

  _____

  _____

- What are the obstacles that will prevent you from reaching your goal?_____

  _____

  _____

- What information and knowledge do you need in order to overcome your obstacles and meet your goal?_____

  _____

  _____

- What people can help you reach your goal? _____

  _____

  _____

Step 5
Take action.

No need for a long explanation here. Step 5 is simply this: *begin carrying out your plan.* At this point, one of two things will happen:

you'll take action
or
you won't take action

If you find that you're able to begin your plan right away, congratulations, you're *already* beginning to turn your goal into a reality! On the other hand, sometimes it's just not that easy to get things going. If that's the case, use this simple formula to help muster up some motivation:

Motivation = Confidence + Importance

The above formula shows us that motivation is made up of confidence and importance. Therefore, to get yourself more motivated to get started, you will either need to increase your confidence that you can actually reach your goal, the importance of reaching you goal, or preferably *both.* A few tips:

- the key to increasing confidence that you can actually reach your goal is by arming yourself with all the necessary tools, skills, and know-how you need to succeed. So, *what information, knowledge or other people do you need in order to overcome your obstacles and make reaching your goal easier?*

- the key to increasing the importance of reaching your goal is to find a reason to get started that gives you something you really want. So, *why did you want to reach this particular goal in the first place?* The more you realize the benefits you will gain by reaching your goal, the more motivated you'll be to get started!

Step 6
Check your progress periodically.

This is a crucial step that involves taking time out now and then to see where you're at in terms of reaching your goal.

Why re-evaluate things? Two main reasons. To show you the progress you're making–which gives you incentive to keep going, *or* to show you the lack of progress you're making–so you can make adjustments to your plan.

Since you've made your goal measurable in some way, it won't be hard to tell if you're moving forward, getting stuck, or going in reverse. A few things to think about as you're taking action and pursuing your goal…

- set up a *regular* time every week or so to check on your progress

- if everything is going according to plan, recognize it–and don't forget to give yourself a pat on the back!

- realize that even *small* steps can bring *big* progress over time. For example, if you lost only one ounce a day, you'd be about two pounds lighter in a month!

- getting discouraged and side-tracked are completely normal. If it happens, concentrate on the progress you've made, make use of the people you identified in Step 4 that can help you reach your goal, and keep reminding yourself of all the benefits of reaching your goal.

- if new obstacles do come up, you might have to revise your plan . Be flexible and make the necessary adjustments to reach your goal.

- if you get stuck on a step, consider breaking that step down into smaller, more manageable steps

```
┌─────────────────────────────────────────┐
│                                         │
│              Step 7                     │
│         Evaluate the Outcome            │
│                                         │
└─────────────────────────────────────────┘
```

When all is said and done, you've either met your goal or you didn't. So that's that, right? Almost. Here are a few things to think about when your goal deadline comes around...

- if you've met your goal, make sure you take some time out and take a good look back at the different steps you took in the process of getting there–that way you can use this same winning approach the next time you pursue a goal.

- if you didn't reach you goal, what obstacles prevented you? What could you have done differently? Recognizing mistakes and adjustments that need to be made will help you out when you go after other goals–or take another stab at the same goal again.

```
┌─────────────────────────────────────────┐
│                                         │
│              Step 8                     │
│              Repeat                     │
│                                         │
└─────────────────────────────────────────┘
```

In the year 1900, the average person lived to be about 47 years old. Today, the average life expectancy of a human being is 78. With people clearly living longer, _continually_ setting and working on self-concordant, intrinsic goals to stay happy is as important as ever for people of _all_ ages. What kinds of things will you fill your days with?

References

It's true! All the information you have just read is based on controlled trials and scientific studies that have been published in peer-reviewed journals. Since I know there are readers out there that like to check out the information for themselves, I've included this reference section.

However unlike most reference sections you see, I've included the page numbers as a way of citing my sources. Why did I do this? Simply because I chose to present the happiness research in an easy-to-digest *story* format, which did not lend itself to citing references with numbers or parentheses–as is customarily done.

And so, with that thought in mind, here's a comprehensive list of supporting references–just so you'll know that I've done my homework *and* so I can give credit where credit is due…

How Happiness Is Scientifically Studied

p. 8   Validity and reliability of happiness scales. Lyubomirsky, S, et al. "A Measure of Subjective Happiness: Preliminary Reliability and Construct Validation" *Social Indicators Research* 1999;46:137-155.

p. 9   Other indicators of happiness. Sandvik, E, et al. "Subjective Well-Being: The Convergence and Stability of Self-Report and Non-Self Report Measures" *Journal of Personality* 1993;61:317- 342.

Things That Have Little To Do
With Long-Term Happiness

p. 12 People in wealthier countries happier. Diener, E, et al. "Factors Predicting the Subjective Well-Being of Nations" *Journal of Personality and Social Psychology* 1995;69:851-864.

p. 13   Happiness and wealth within a single country. Diener, E, et al.
"Happiness of the Very Wealthy" *Social Indicators Research*
1985;16:263-274.

p. 13 .12 correlation between income and happiness within a single
country. Diener, E, et al. "The Relationship Between Income and
Subjective Well-Being: Relative or Absolute?" *Social Indicators
Research* 1993;28:195-223.

p. 13 .13 correlation between income and happiness within nineteen nations.
Diener, E, et al. "Will Money Increase Subjective Well-Being?"
Social Indicators Research 2002;57:123.

p. 14   Income increase and happiness in the United States, Japan, and
France. Diener, E, et al. "Measuring Quality of Life: Economic,
Social, and Subjective Indicators" *Social Indicators Research*
1997;40:189-216.

p. 14   Lottery winners and happiness levels. Brickman, P, et al. "Lottery
Winners and Accident Victims: Is Happiness Relative?" *Journal of
Personality and Social Psychology* 1978;36:917-927.

p. 15   Happiness of millionaires, the Amish, and the Maasai. Diener, E, et al.
"Beyond Money. Toward an Economy of Well-Being" *Psychological
Science in the Public Interest* 2004;5:1-31.

p. 17   Cross-sectional study on aging and happiness. Carstensen, L, et al.
"Emotional Experience in Everyday Life Across the Adult Life Span"
Journal of Personality and Social Psychology 2000;79:644-655.

p. 18 Longitudinal study on aging and happiness. Charles, S, et al. "Age-Related Differences and Change in Positive and Negative Affect Over 23 Years" *Journal of Personality and Social Psychology* 2001;80:136-151.

p. 19 Health and happiness. Brief, A, et al. "Integrating Bottom-Up and Top-Down Theories of Subjective Well-Being: The Case of Health" *Journal of Personality and Social Psychology* 1993;64:646-653.

p. 20 Health and happiness. Okun, M, et al. "Physician and Self-Ratings of Health, Neuroticism and Subjective Well-Being Among Men and Women" *Personality and Individual Differences* 1984;5:533-539.

p. 20 Disability and happiness in 60 plus year olds. Schneider, G, et al. "Old and Ill and Still Feeling Well? Determinants of Subjective Well-Being in ≥60 Year Olds: The Role of the Sense of Coherence" *Am J Geriatr Psychiatry* 2006;14:850-859.

p. 20 Happiness and the legally blind. Feinman, S. "The Blind as 'Ordinary People'" *Journal of Visual Impairment and Blindness* 1978;72:231-238.

p. 21 Happiness and spinal cord injury. Dijkers, M. "Quality of Life of Individuals with Spinal Cord Injury: A Review of Conceptualization, Measurement, and Research Findings" *Journal of Rehabilitation Research and Development* 2005;42:87-110.

p. 23 Happiness levels in men and women in 16 nations. Inglehart, R. 1990 *Culture Shift In Advanced Industrial Society* Princeton: Princeton University Press (p. 220).

p. 23 Other studies on gender and happiness. Fujita, F, et al. "Gender Differences in Negative Affect and Well-Being: The Case for Emotional Intensity" *Journal of Personality and Social Psychology* 1991;61:427-434.

p. 23 Intelligence and happiness. Watten, R, et al. "Quality of Life, Intelligence and Mood" *Social Indicators Research* 1995;36:287-299.

p. 23 Other studies on intelligence and happiness. Palmore, E. "Predictors of Successful Aging" *The Gerontologist* 1979;19:427-431.

p. 23 Other studies on intelligence and happiness. Palmore, E, et al. "Health and Social Factors Related to Life Satisfaction" *Journal of Health and Social Behavior* 1972;13:68-80.

p. 23 Other studies on intelligence and happiness. Sigelman, L. "Is Ignorance Bliss? A Reconsideration of the Folk Wisdom" *Human Relations* 1981;34:965-974.

Things That Have A Lot To Do
With Long-Term Happiness

p. 25 Three things that contribute to long-term happiness. Lyubomirsky, S, et al. "Pursuing Happiness: The Architecture of Sustainable Change" *Review of General Psychology* 2005;9:111-131.

p. 26 Happiness and genetics. Tellegen, A, et al. "Personality Similarity in Twins Reared Apart and Together" *Journal of Personality and Social Psychology* 1988;54:1031-1039.

p. 26 Happiness and genetics. Lykken, D, et al. "Happiness is a Stochastic Phenomenon" *Psychological Science* 1996;7:186-189.

p. 26 Happiness and genetics. Nes, R, et al. "Subjective Well-Being: Genetic and Environmental Contributions to Stability and Change" *Psychological Medicine* 2006;36:1033-1042.

p. 27 Loss of spouse and happiness. Lucas, R, et al. "Re-examining Adaptation and the Set Point Model of Happiness: Reactions to Changes In Marital Status" *Journal of Personality and Social Psychology* 2003;84:527-539.

p. 27 Divorce and happiness. Lucas, R. "Time Does Not Heal All Wounds. A Longitudinal Study of Reaction and Adaptation to Divorce" *Psychological Science* 2005;16:945-950.

p. 27 Unemployment and happiness. Lucas, R, et al. "Unemployment Alters the Set Point for Life Satisfaction" *Psychological Science* 2004;15:8-13.

How To Find Long-Term Happiness

p. 32 Randomized controlled trial showing long-term increases in happiness. Green, L, et al. "Cognitive-Behavioral, Solution-Focused Life Coaching: Enhancing Goal Striving, Well-Being, and Hope" *The Journal of Positive Psychology* 2006;1:142-149.

p. 33 Controlled trial showing long-term increases in happiness. Dube, M, et al. "Impact of a Personal Goals Management Program on the Subjective Well-Being of Young Retirees" *Revue Europeenne de Psychologie Appliquee* 2007;57:183-192.

p. 35 People with self-concordant goals are happier. Sheldon, K, et al. "Goal Striving, Need Satisfaction, and Longitudinal Well-Being: The Self-Concordance Model" *Journal of Personality and Social Psychology* 1999;76:482-497.

p. 35 People with self-concordant goals are happier. Sheldon, K, et al. "Pursuing Personal Goals: Skills Enable Progress, But Not All Progress Is Beneficial" *Personality and Social Psychology Bulletin* 1998;24:1319-1331.

p. 36 The association between self-concordant goals and happiness is universal. Sheldon, K, et al. "Self-Concordance and Subjective Well-Being in Four Cultures" *Journal of Cross-Cultural Psychology* 2004;35:209-223.

p. 37 Descriptions of intrinsic and extrinsic goals. Kasser, T. "Personal Aspirations, the 'Good Life' and the Law" *Deakin Law Review* 2005;10:34-5.

p. 39 People with intrinsic goals are happier. Sheldon, K, et al. "The Independent Effects of Goal Contents and Motives on Well-Being: It's Both What Your Pursue and Why You Pursue It" *Personality and Social Psychology Bulletin* 2004;30:475-486.

p. 39 The association between intrinsic goals and happiness is universal. Ryan, R, et al. "The American Dream in Russia: Extrinsic Aspirations and Well-Being in Two Cultures" *Personality and Social Psychology Bulletin* 1999;25:1509-1524.

p. 39 The association between intrinsic goals and happiness is universal. Schmuck, P, et al. "Intrinsic and Extrinsic Goals: Their Structure and Relationship to Well-Being in German and U.S. College Students" *Social Indicators Research* 2000;50:225-241.

p. 40 Intrinsic and self-concordant goal contents make individual contributions to happiness. Sheldon, K, et al. "The Independent Effects of Goal Contents and Motives on Well-Being: It's Both What Your Pursue and Why You Pursue It" *Personality and Social Psychology Bulletin* 2004;30:475-486.

A Step-by-Step Plan

p. 50 Qualities of self-concordant and non-concordant goals. Sheldon, K, et al. "Self-Concordance and Subjective Well-Being in Four Cultures" *Journal of Cross-Cultural Psychology* 2004;35:214.

p. 51 Qualities of intrinsic and extrinsic goals. Kasser, T. "Personal Aspirations, the 'Good Life' and the Law" *Deakin Law Review* 2005;10:34-5.

p. 55 Human life expectancies. *www.cdc.gov*

HAPPINESS

Printed in the United States
142910LV00005B/2/P